THIS BOOK BELONGS TO:

_____

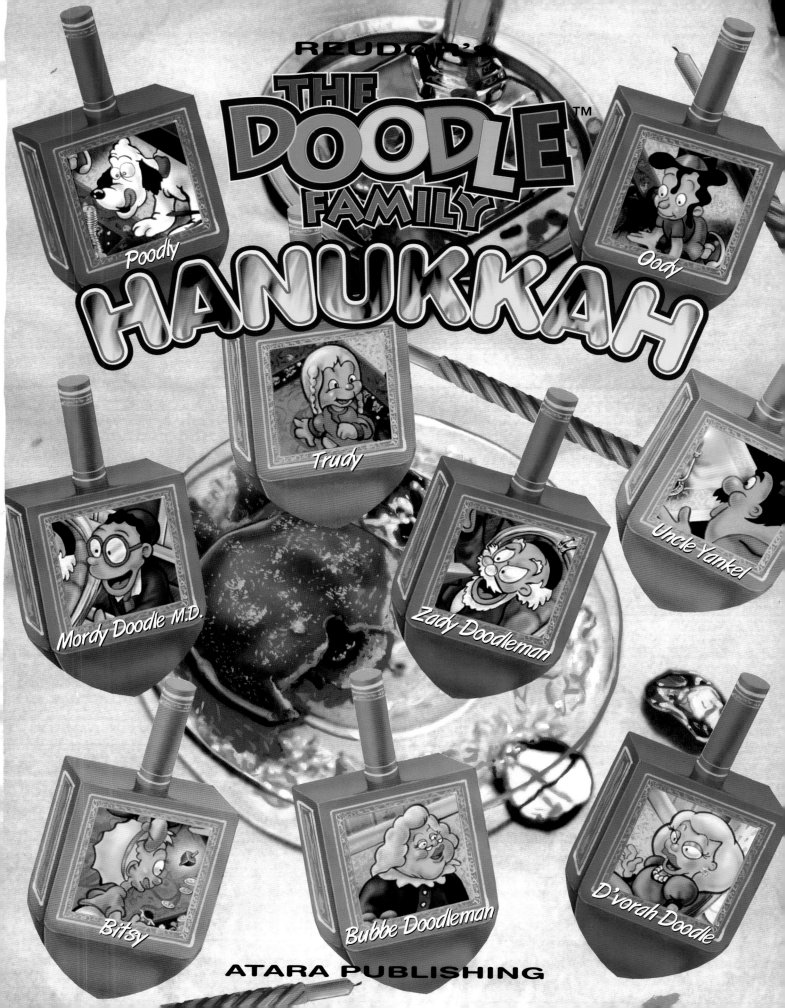

This book was made possible by the joint efforts of

Jeff "Magik Mouse" Coen - Graphic Design
"Jumpin' Josh Flash" Coen - Verbiage
Burt "Offerings" Griswold - Inkiage
Jack "The Black" Knight - MasterPainter
Baron Vohn Mrkva - Lettererer
Sheina "Rebel" Berkowitz - Prooofing
The Doodles (Effie & Cari & Ariel & Shira & Gilad)

This book was almost made impossible by

Ridiculous deadlines
Great beach weather
A bizarre occasional need for sleep
Nagging phone calls
Daniel "The Transylvanian" Ardel

Printed in Hong Kong

ISBN 1-886611-11-4
Library of Congress Number 96-084247

North American Distribution by Alef Judaica, Inc.
Culver City, California
Published by Atara Publishing
Huntington Beach, California.

1-888-DOODLES
the_doodles@earthlink.net
http://www.doodles.com

FORWARD
by Dr. Laura Schlessinger

A people are defined by their beliefs and known for their behaviors. The solidarity and energy of a group of people is supported by its history, conferred through spoken and written legends, stories, and myths. They are not always meant to be exact, they are meant to be exalting. In modern times the search for knowledge, profound levels of understanding and the effort required for specialness have been sacrificed to the idols of expediency and superficial contentment. This is an important time in the ongoing history of the Jewish People. We need renewal - we need our stories again to be an important part of our lives.

I welcome the DOODLE FAMILY into this effort. I am enthralled with the possibilities of learning about Jewish history, law and life through this engaging family. One might be concerned that a cartoon mode of expression would diminish or detract from the deep meaning of the stories behind Jewish thought and life - worry not. Reudor is a wonderful and sensitive artist who has the marvelous ability to express the profound through the playful, making **THE DOODLE FAMILY HANUKKAH** a fascinating experience for all ages. It includes a comic book of adventure and fun through which modern Israel as well as the ancient one become very real to the children so far from Jerusalem.

Traditions have become secularized and trivialized in our current, more materialistic than spiritual atmosphere, and have therefore lost much of their point, which is to inspire and direct. THE DOODLE FAMILY series of books accomplishes the opposite: through the explanation of customs and traditions practiced and observed by Jews from all the world, Reudor helps to renew our sense of respect and awe about our history. We are part of an incredible 4,000 year family - celebrate it with the DOODLE FAMILY.

Laura C. Schlessinger

Author: HOW COULD YOU DO THAT?!
    The Abdication of Character, Courage, and Conscience
    Harper-Collins, 1996.

    TEN STUPID THINGS WOMEN DO TO MESS UP THEIR LIVES.
    Random House, 1994

Where To FIND what.

JUG of OIL:
For every hidden jug of oil you find in this book, you get a latke. Then look for the stomach pump.
(find 8 more jugs of oil hidden in this book)

WhatsInAName?

Everyone knows the basic story of Hanukkah, but at times events seem a little confusing due to use of certain words and phrases. Let's try and see who is who and what is what:

The bad guys

The Hellenists were Jews who accepted the Greek culture and assimilated. They changed their traditions, dress and language, adopting words like sanhedrin and synagogue. Joshua became Jason, Eliakim became Alcimus. (Not unlike when Jewish converts to christianity aided the Catholic church in debating rabbis during the Middle Ages, and Jewish kapos assisted the Nazis in the concentration camps.) We refer to their masters by three names: Seleucids - after Alexander's general, Seleucus, who became ruler of Syria; Syrians - Because of their country of origin; Greeks - as they followed Greek culture.

Oody has another name for them: JERKS!!

IT'S ALL GREEK TO ME!

The Good guys

The Hasidim (no relation to today's Hassidic Jews) continued embracing the Torah amidst pressures to assimilate. The Hasmonean family, headed by the priest Mattathias, were Hasidim. They came from the town of Modin to lead the Jewish people in a quest to free Judea of Greek influence and rule. The Hasmoneans ruled Judea for more than 200 years. They were also called Maccabees: As Mattathias led his followers he proclaimed, "Mi kamokha ba'elim Adonai," meaning *who is like you among the gods, Lord?* The Hebrew acronym is Maccabee! Another reason for the name may be the actual Hebrew meaning of the word, *hammer*, referring to Judah's strength with which he slammed the enemy.

Years before the holiday was referred to as Hanukkah, it was called the Festival of Lights. Josephus said it was because the free practice of religion was to the Jews like the rising light of day. The Gemara says it's simply because of the miracle of the oil and the light that lasted eight days. It is also called the Feast of Fire.

Some commentators divide the Hebrew word Hanukkah this way: **hanu - kkah:** *hanu – (rested) kh – (the Hebrew letters stand for 25). They ceased fighting on the 25th of Kislev and thus Hanukkah marks this victory.*

LIGHTS *MENORAH* *ACTION!*

What you'll need to celebrate Hanukkah:

Hanukkiyah (menorah)

Draydels

Matches

Chocolate gelt

צדקה

TZEDAKAH

Tzedakah box

Traditional Holiday foods

Candles (or Oil and wicks) for eight days

Lighting your Hanukkiyah:

After sunset...

1. Set a candle or wick in the higher holder. It's called the shamash.
2. Place a candle for the first night in the far right holder.
3. Light the shamash and say the holiday blessings.

On first night, say (see page 12):

- L'hadlik ner shel Hanukkah
- Sheh'asah nissim la'avoteinu
- Sheheheyanu

The rest of the nights just say first two.

4. Light the first candle with the shamash, then replace it in its holder.

5. Each night after, repeat steps 1- 3 and add one candle to the left until the eighth night when the whole hanukkiyah is filled up! Using the shamash, light the newest candle first.

6. Place your hanukkiyah in the window or in the front doorway opposite the mezuzah so you can share the mitzvah with others.

7. Sing Ha-neirot Hallalu, Maoz Tzur and other songs.

Additional customs are followed in different communities:
Some prayer books contain Megilat Antiochus, which considers Jonathan, rather than Judah, the main hero, and recently the Conservative Rabbinical Assembly published Megilat Hanukkah which contains versions of the book of Maccabees I and II. Sephardic Jews say Psalm 30: "Mizmor Shir Hanukkat ha-Bayit L'David": A Psalm for the dedication of the Temple, by David.

The Two Miracles o

There were several Greek decrees against the Jews that stood out:

1. The law against observing the Shabbat, when we affirm that the world was created in six days and we rest on the seventh.

2. The law banning celebrating Rosh Chodesh (the new month), signifying that time serves a holy purpose.

3. The law outlawing circumcision, which was a sign the Jewish body and soul are holy.

4. The law that all Jewish female brides-to-be would have to have relations with a Greek officer before marriage — an attempt to destroy the sanctity of the Jewish people.

Until the Middle Ages, the focus of Hanukkah remained on the miracle of the oil. Megilat Antiochus shows Jonathan, rather than Judah, the main hero. Today the text of this scroll is available in some prayer books. Also, the Book of the Maccabees I and II were once available only to non-Jewish readers. Recently,

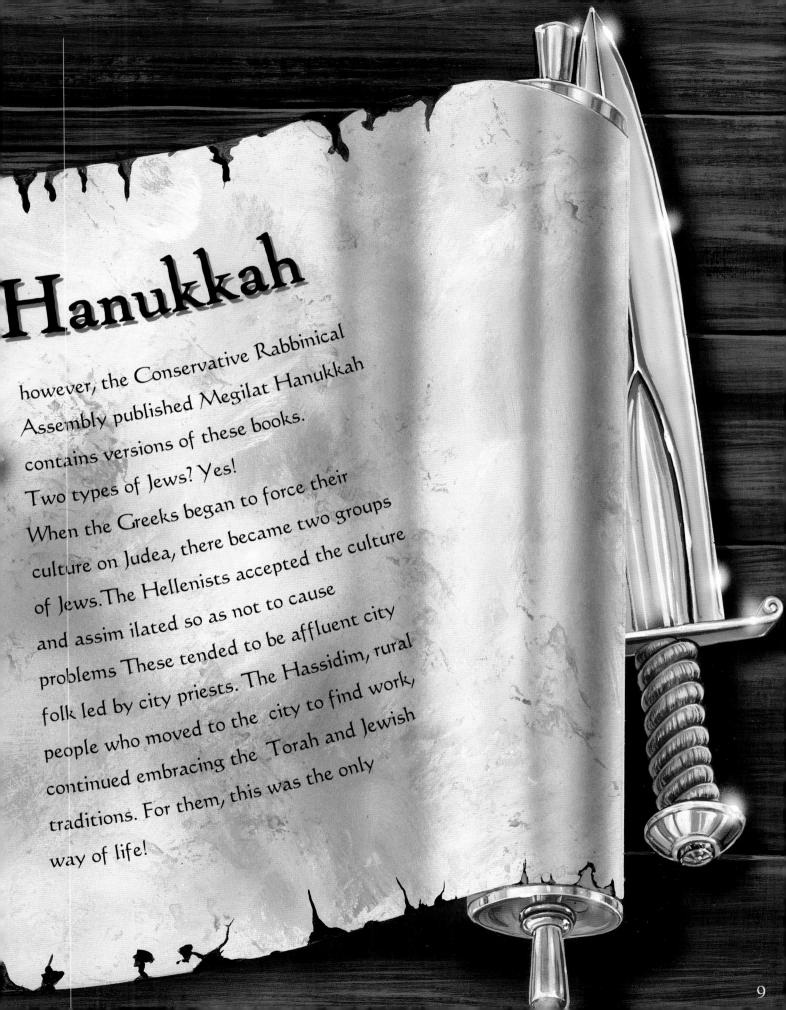

Hanukkah

however, the Conservative Rabbinical Assembly published Megilat Hanukkah contains versions of these books.

Two types of Jews? Yes! When the Greeks began to force their culture on Judea, there became two groups of Jews. The Hellenists accepted the culture and assim ilated so as not to cause problems These tended to be affluent city folk led by city priests. The Hassidim, rural people who moved to the city to find work, continued embracing the Torah and Jewish traditions. For them, this was the only way of life!

THE MACCABEAN EPIC

The Reign of Alexander (336-323 BCE)

- **Alexander the Great**, king of Macedonia, conquers much of the known world, including Judea.

- He permits Jews throughout his empire to observe Judaism and **Simon the Just**, High Priest and spiritual leader, promises that all Jewish boys born that year would be named Alexander.

- At just 33, Alexander dies, sending his kingdom into chaos. His five generals battle continuously for ever greater portions of his empire.

The Jews under Egyptian Rule (312-198 BCE)

- The Egyptian king, **Ptolemy I**, now rules Judea and southern Syria. Many Jews move from the Holy Land to Egypt.

- Jews in Judea and Egypt adopt Greek ideas, language — even names. These followers of Greek culture, called Hellenism, become know as Hellenists.

- The creation of the Septuagint, along with increased assimilation, causes many Jews to lose touch with their heritage completely.

- During the Battle of Paneion, **Antiochus III**, the Seleucid ruler of Syria, defeated Egypt and gained control of Judea.

Jerusalem under Antiochus (175-167 BCE)

- **King Antiochus Epiphanes** appoints **Jason** and later **Menelaos** to the High Priest post in exchange for money and the promise of Hellenizing all of Jerusalem.

- Antiochus storms Jerusalem with his troops and slaughters 40,000 men, women, and children. He ransacks the Temple's treasures and converts the House of God into a pagan temple.

The Maccabean Uprising (166-164 BCE)

- **Apelles**, a royal official, sets up an alter to Jupiter in the town of Modin. When a Jew agrees to sacrifice on it, the priest **Mattathias the Hasmonean**, kills the traitor. With his five sons, he kills Apelles and many of his soldiers, then escapes to the Gophna hills.

- More Jews join the Hasmoneans, forge weapons and learn guerrilla warfare. Mattathias dies. Under the spiritual leadership of **Simon** and the military leadership of **Judah**, their numbers grow and they vanquish their oppressors in night attacks.

- The small rebel army emerges victorious when they face **Apollonius** and **Seron**, two Syrian generals, and their superior forces.

- **Lysias**, Antiochus' top commander, sends his generals, **Nicanor**, **Gorgias**, and **Ptolemy**, and more than 120,000 troops against Judah's 6,000 men. Yet, the Jewish army triumphs. Lysias returns personally, but is thoroughly beaten in Bet-Tzur near Hebron.

The Dedication of the Temple (25 Kislev, 164 BCE)

- Judah reclaims and restores the desecrated temple. We commemorate this event each year with our celebration of Hanukkah.

The Maccabean Wars Continue (164-135 BCE)

- Antiochus dies, insane. Judah and his brothers set out to secure Judea's borders. They battle and decimate the Idumeans, Amonites, local Greeks, and the Philistines.

- Lysias returns with a massive army, and **Eleazar**, the youngest Maccabee brother, dies under the elephant (see pg. 47). At the end of the battle, a peace treaty is signed.

- Judah claims victory at Bet-Choron and destroys the arrogant general, Nicanor.

- 160 BCE: **Bacchides** attacks Judah's unprepared battalion of 800 men with his 22,000 troops. Near Adasa, an arrow pierces Judah's armor, ending the life of one of the greatest Jewish heroes of all time.

- Arab assassins murder **Jochanan**, the eldest brother. **Jonathan** defeats Bacchides and forces **King Demetrius** to agree to a peace treaty and recognize Jonathan as governor.

- **Alexander Balas** overthrows Demetrius and becomes king. He proclaims Jonathan High Priest. Eight years later, Jonathan is tricked by the new ruler, **Tryphon**, and is taken prisoner and murdered.

- Simon liberates Judea and is proclaimed Prince and High Priest. Antiochus bribes Simon's brother-in-law to murder the Jewish leader, spelling the end for the last Maccabee brother. Simon is buried in the family tomb in Modin, along with his father and brothers. His son **Jochanan Hyrkanus** becomes leader.

Every year on the first night of Hanukkah, in the legendary town of Modin, Jews light a torch at the Maccabee family tomb. The torch is relayed in a running race to Jerusalem and then to other parts of country.

ברוך אתה יי, אלהינו מלך העולם,
אשר קדשנו במצותיו, וצונו להדליק נר של חנכה.

Baruch atah Adonai, Eloheinu Melech ha-olam,
asher kidshanu bemitzvotav,
vetzivanu lehadlik neyr shel Chanukah.

Blessed are You, HASHEM our GOD, King of the universe, who has sanctified us by His commandments and commanded us to kindle the Hanukkah lights.

The 1st Night

ברוך אתה יי, אלהינו מלך העולם,
שעשה נסים לאבותינו בימים ההם בזמן הזה.

Baruch atah Adonai, Eloheinu Melech ha-olam,
she-asa nisim la-avoteynu bayamim ha-heym bazman hazeh.

Blessed are You, HASHEM our GOD, King of the universe, who performed miraculous deeds for our ancestors in days of old, at this season.

recite on the first day only

ברוך אתה יי, אלהינו מלך העולם,
שהחינו וקימנו והגיענו לזמן הזה.

Baruch atah Adonai, Eloheinu Melech ha-olam,
she-hecheyanu vekiy'manu vehigianu lazman hazeh.

Blessed are You, HASHEM our GOD, King of the universe, for giving us life, for sustaining us, and for enabling us to reach this season.

THE DRAYDEL DEPARTMENT

The game of Draydel was used during the rule of Antiochus Epiphanes before the Maccabee revolt. During this time, any Jew who studied Torah was executed. So, when they gathered to study, they all had a Draydel top ready for action in case soldiers should come by! (These days, it's the other way around: if you're playing Draydel when you should be doing homework, you have to quickly put your Draydel away when your parents come by).

Merchants brought Draydels from India to Europe during the Middle Ages. Germans adopted the custom of playing the Draydel game, and created the traditional markings, N, G, H, S, which stood for Nichts (nothing), Ganz (all), Halb (half), and Stell ein (put in). They also named the game, calling it "drehen" meaning turn. The game became so popular, children throughout Europe used to cast their own draydels out of lead.

In Hebrew, the Draydel is called a S'vivon (spinner). The German markings were changed to Hebrew. Nun, Gimel, Heh, Shin stand for Ness, Gadol, Ha-ya, Sham: "a great miracle happened there." In Israel, they change "there" to "here," since the miracle happened in the Holy Land.

It all adds up: Each letter, Nun, Gimel, Heh, Shin, has a numeric value. Add 'em up and it equals the same value as the word "Mashiach" – the Messiah.

The 2nd Night

15

THE DOODLE FAMILY Adventures!
THE YOUNG MACCABEES

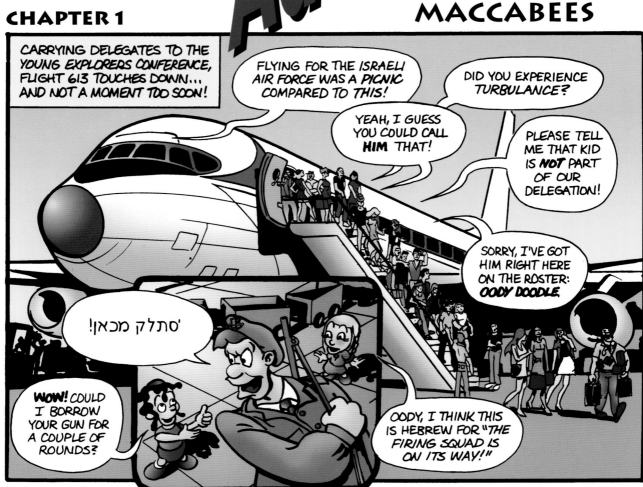

19

THE GAMING COMMISSION

Traditional Draydel

Give 10-15 pennies, nuts, raisins, or other fun items to each player.

Everyone then puts one item in the middle, called "the pot."

Taking turns, players spin the draydel and act according to whichever side lands up. Spin a Nun and you get "nothing" from the pot. Gimel means "take all"; Heh means "take half;" and Shin means "put one in."

When only one item remains in the pot, each player contributes one item. When an odd number is left, the player who spins Heh takes half plus one. When one player wins all the items from all the other players in the game, the game is over.

Draydel Blaster!

Everyone spins a draydel, trying to knock down the other draydels. The last to remain spinning wins.

ANYONE FOR A GAME OF **DRAYDEL BLASTER?...** ANYONE !?

Card Games

Playing cards is also a custom on Hanukkah. Since traditionally the professional gambler was looked down upon, some communities put a ban on this form of gambling for the entire year except during Hanukkah. Because of the importance of the number 8 on Hanukkah, Crazy Eights is a fun card game to play. Also, check out *Oodles of Doodles for Hanukkah* activity book for a customized Hanukkah card game!

Chess and Checkers

Make one side the Macabbees and the other, the Syrian-Greeks. Let the battle rage on!

Search!

Using clues supplied by the host, different teams embark on a search for a jug of oil. The losing team uses the oil to fry latkes, which makes everyone a winner!

The third night of Hanukkah is connected to the light of truth which is brought about by the thanksgiving and praise we give on Hanukkah. According to Rabbi Nachman of Breslov, this light is brought about by three rays of truth: true prayer, learning Torah in truth, and marriage unions formed in truth.

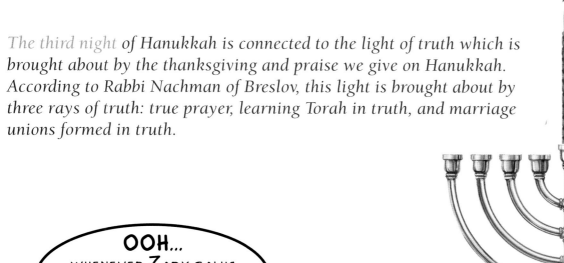

Simon the Just, was the High Priest and Judea's spiritual leader. He refused to sever ties with Persia and pledge allegiance and money to **Alexander the Great**.

Alexander vowed revenge and advanced angrily on Jerusalem. Simon boldly lead a great procession to meet him. Upon seeing him, instead of unleashing his wrath, Alexander saluted the High Priest, explaining to his generals that this was the holy man who appeared in his dreams and encouraged him in his victories.

Alexander permited Jews throughout his empire to observe Judaism. In return, Simon promised that all Jewish boys born that year would be named Alexander.

Let There Be Lights!

The candelabra we use to commemorate Hanukkah is called a hanukkiyah. It's adapted from the ancient menorah in the Temple which was fashioned after the Tree of Life in the Garden of Eden. It had seven branches representing the seven days of creation. However, today's hanukkiyah has nine branches - eight to signify the miracle and one to light them all. Legend has it that the first hanukkiah was crafted from eight metal spears found in the Temple.

Altogether there are 36 candles lit on Hanukkah, the exact number of hours Adam spent in the Garden of Eden before being banished. The connection? The lights of Hanukkah are considered a spark of the original light of the Garden of Eden. Until the redemption the Garden will remain hidden from us, and no work may be done by the light of the candles as we reflect on the joy to come.

According to tradition, the menorah at the Temple illuminated the whole world. King Solomon built the Temple's windows just for this purpose. The windows were wide on the inside and narrow on the outside, not to catch the light from the outside as normal windows do, but rather to project the light of the menorah outward to the world.

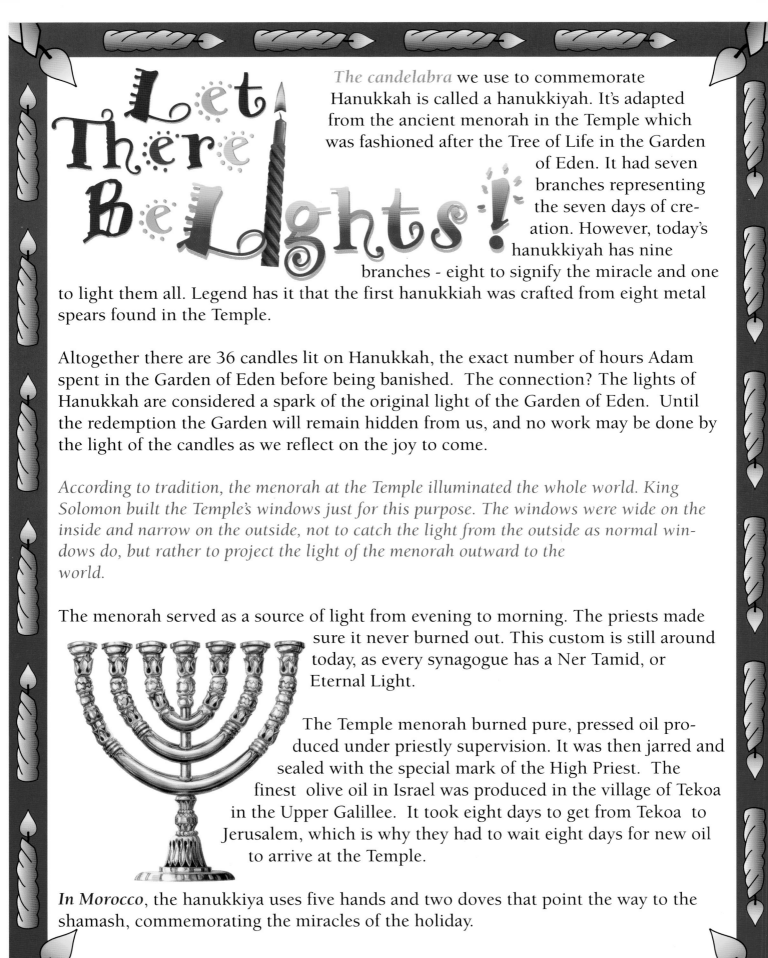

The menorah served as a source of light from evening to morning. The priests made sure it never burned out. This custom is still around today, as every synagogue has a Ner Tamid, or Eternal Light.

The Temple menorah burned pure, pressed oil produced under priestly supervision. It was then jarred and sealed with the special mark of the High Priest. The finest olive oil in Israel was produced in the village of Tekoa in the Upper Galillee. It took eight days to get from Tekoa to Jerusalem, which is why they had to wait eight days for new oil to arrive at the Temple.

In Morocco, the hanukkiya uses five hands and two doves that point the way to the shamash, commemorating the miracles of the holiday.

Jews who fled persecution in Spain in the late 1400s and went to Syria, began the custom of lighting two shamash candles, reminding them of the extra amount of protection they received during their journey to their new land. In later years, a similar tradition was adopted by Turkish Jews who had moved to Syria. Initially the Syrian Jews didn't quite trust the kashrut of the new immigrants. After some time, however, they accepted them into the community and the Turkish Jews were so grateful, they lit another light!

The Syrian Jews themselves didn't even use a shamash. The synagogue's shamash (Hebrew for caretaker) gave each family a decorated candle to use in lighting the hanukkiyah.

The branches must form a straight line so that people passing by can tell which night of Hanukkah it is. Some people used to add a back wall to the hanukkiyah so they could mount it on their porches safely. In Yemen each boy lit his own hanukkiyah and placed it on the wall. When he grew up and married, he took it with him to start his own Hanukkah wall.

Today, public menorah lightings have become popularized in America by the Chabad movement, as the menorah is a symbol of religious tolerance and a contrast between the light of morality and the darkness of immorality and paganism. One is even lit each year on the lawn of the White House!

The great scholars Shammai and Hillel disagree on which flame to light first. Shammai says all eight lights should be kindled on the first night and then one less each night after. Hillel says that since the purpose of the holiday is to increase our joy, we start with one light on first night and add a new one each night after.

The great Maimonides believed the simple act of lighting was the most important of all. He said that even if a person has no food to eat, he should beg or sell his garments in order to buy oil and lamps to light them.

In Amsterdam during World War II, Anne Frank and her family hid from the Nazis in a tiny attic and celebrated by exchanging little presents. Other Jews in the concentration camps saved bits of butter or fat for candles, old potatoes as stands, and clothing threads as wicks to be able to light the hanukkiyahs.

The book of Proverbs tells us that "A lamp of God is the soul of man". The soul is likened to the Menorah, which explains why the oil, representing the Divine Wisdom, must be pure.

Another appropriate name for Hanukkah should have been the Music Festival - it seems more songs have been written for this one holiday than all others combined. When Judah Maccabee's bravery caught the imagination of the people of Judea, songs were sung in his praise, as in the case of King David: "He was like a lion in his deeds, like a lion's cub roaring for prey."

Ma'oz Tzur, Rock of Ages, is a hymn composed between the 11th and 13th century by a poet named Mordecai. Its popular melody was adopted in the 15th century from a German folksong.

In Yemen, children used to wear blue clothing during the holiday because the heavens are blue and miracles are from the heavens. In school, the children re-created the winning Maccabbean battle. They read Megilat Antiochus, sang and played games and then marched through the streets, stopping at each house to greet their neighbors.

In 1747 George Friederic Handel, the famous English composer, composed an oratorio called Judas Maccabeus. It was first performed at the Covent Garden Theatre in London.

In Venice, Jews travel the canals in gondolas and stop at every house that's illuminated with Hanukkah lights. They extend holiday greetings in joyous songs to the neighbors they meet.

One of the catchiest tunes for the holiday is "My Dreydl" by Samuel Grossman. Our Doodles have their own version (as I'm sure does each of you!), but first here's the original:

I have a little dreydl
I made it out of clay;
And when it's dry and ready
Then dreydl I shall play.

O dreydl, dreydl, dreydl,
I made it out of clay;
O dreydl, dreydl, dreydl,
Now dreydl I shall play.

My dreydl is always playful,
It loves to dance and spin.
A happy game of dreydl,
Come play, now let's begin.

It has a lovely body,
With leg so short and thin;
And when it is all tired,
It drops and then I win.

The Meaning of Hanukkah According to Uncle Yankel

A Play in 1 Act, 4 Scenes, for 8 nights, with 9 players, and lotsa nonsense

Mom:	What's going on here?
Kids:	Uncle Yankel is telling us Hanukkah stories.
Dad:	That ought to be good! I'll get the popcorn.
Bubbe:	I'll bring around the sufganiyot.
Mom:	Be sure your stories are rated G, Yankel!
Dad:	Most science fiction tales are.
Zady:	Nu? You're waiting, maybe, for Mashiach?
Yankel:	I'm waiting for all my detractors to have their say…
Poodly:	Arf!
Yankel:	Okay, I guess that's everyone.

* * *

Yankel:	Mm, delicious sufganiyot, Bubbe! Speaking of Sufganiyot, let me tell you how I originated these scrumptious jelly donuts, a tradition since followed by Jews everywhere!
Oody:	C'mon, Uncle Yankel, people have been eating sufganiyot forever!
Trudy:	Fried foods are a reminder of the oil used to light the menorah in theTemple!
Yankel:	Exactly! See, as a kid I used to work at Blumbergstein's Donut Shop. At Hanukkah time everyone in the neighborhood would stop by to buy glazed donuts for the holiday. Well, on the day before Hanukkah, we ran out of holes!
Everyone:	You WHAT?!?
Poodly:	Arf??
Yankel:	Sure! Do you think the holes get into the donuts by themselves? Of course not, people put them there! Well, we ran out. What a terrible scene it was. I mean, can you imagine Hanukkah without donuts? Unthinkable!
Zady:	I never understood why people say Bubbe Meises. It should be Yankel Meises!
Bitsy:	What's Bubbe Meises?
Oody:	That's the holes without the donuts!
Bitsy:	Oh…
Yankel:	Anyway, I just happened to have some jars of raspberry jam which Bubbe made for me to deliver to Doodleman's Deli after work, and Bubbe's jam was to die for!
Bubbe:	That part is true!
Yankel:	So instead of holes, I filled the donuts with jam, everyone loved them, and this is why we call them Sufganiyot!
Everyone:	Why?!?
Yankel:	Poodly!! (the dog grabs the last two sufganiyot off the table and dashes off)

* * *

Dad:	Hey, bro, maybe you should tell about the fire…
Oody:	COOL! What fire?

Mom:	G rating also means no fire stories!
Yankel:	Not to worry, D'vorah! This is a story of true heroism!
Zady:	Oy vey!
Yankel:	In our neighborhood there were many warehouses and many fires would break out. Civil minded as I am, I joined the volunteer fire department.
Zady:	Oy vey, again!
Bitsy:	Why does Zady keep saying "oy vey?"
Dad:	It beats anything I could come up with.
Yankel:	One evening I was on the way home when I saw a building with flames coming out of the third floor window. There was no time to lose, I jumped on the water pipe and climbed up the wall!
Oody:	Like Spiderman!
Dad:	More like The Incredible Bulk!
Yankel:	I shall ignore these comments.
Bubbe:	Sure, like you ignore reality!
Trudy:	C'mon, Uncle Yankel, you're just making this all up!
Dad:	Actually, Trudy, dear, he did climb the water pipe...
Kids:	?!?!?
Dad:	Down, as he was escaping from Zady after having set the drapes on fire while lighting the menorah!

31

33

The 4th Night

Hanukkah's importance outside of Israel has grown out of proportion to its role as a minor holiday. This is mostly due to the fact that public schools and the media draw a correlation between Hanukkah and Xmas. Instead, we should try to focus on the many other Jewish festivals and traditions. How do some of the other holidays relate to Hanukkah?

Asking God's forgiveness on **Yom Kippur** helps us experience the holiness of Hanukkah. The reason is that on Hanukkah we draw the sanctity of the Holy Temple on ourselves, and this can only take place when our sins are forgiven.

Originally, **Sukkot** was celebrated in the Month of Kislev since Jews weren't able to observe the holiday while the Temple was in enemy hands. When the Temple was liberated, Jews resumed celebration and observed Hanukkah for eight days, just like Sukkot - They even carried lulavim and etrogim! We no longer do this today, but still recite Hallel every day to preserve the connection with Sukkot. In Turkey, they weaved candlewicks from fibers in which the Sukkot Etrog was wrapped. After Hanukkah, the candle remains were formed into another candle which was used for searching for chametz before **Passover**, extending the holiday spirit throughout the year.

According to the Kabbalah, the human being is divided into three sections: head, body and limbs. Both Hanukkah and **Purim** are connected to the limbs, as they reach out close to the world; both are celebrated during the winter; both are considered minor holidays, as their observance was not commanded by the bible, but rather by rabbinical decree; and during the Amida prayer on both holidays, Al Hanisim(For the Miracles) is recited. On the 13th day of Adar , Judah claimed victory in the battle of Bet-Choron and destroyed the armies of the arrogant general Nicanor who vowed to convert the Temple to a shrine for the Greek god Dyonisius. For centuries this day was celebrated as Nicanor Day until the tradition of the Fast of Esther took hold on this day - the day before Purim.

"UNLIKE MANY JEWISH HOLIDAYS, DURING HANUKKAH WE ARE NOT COMMANDED TO DRINK WINE, HOWEVER, WE ARE NOT COMMANDED NOT TO!!! So LeChaim!"

Both Hanukkah and **Shavuot** carry a tradition of eating cheese blintzes and other dairy foods.

The Gemara mentions only the miracle of the oil and not the battles. In fact, the word "Hanukkah" didn't appear in the Talmud until hundreds of years after the miracle happened! The reason the story was censored may have been **Lag B'omer**: since the Gemara was written during Roman rule and after Bar Kokhva's revolt where hundreds of thousand of Jews were killed, the rabbis wanted to discourage Jews from gaining inspiration from the story of the Maccabees and revolt again.

According to the Zohar, during **Rosh Hashana** we connect with the source of energy which enables us to last another year. However, if a person fails to make the connection, Hanukkah offers another opportunity to tap into this divine energy.

In Middle Eastern countries Jewish parents gave their children candles shaped like a hand, called hamsa (five in Arabic), to keep away the evil eye and bring a miracle of protection.

In eastern Europe, the fifth night of Hanukkah is the special one. On that evening, the family prepares a feast and celebrate how light triumphed over darkness since five candles are lit and only three still remain in darkness.

The 5th Night

DELICIOUS • DELIGHTFUL • DELATKES •

A similar custom is found in Syria - a custom so delicious, kids from all over the world beg their parents to adopt it: Instead of a traditional holiday meal, they have a sweet table stacked high with pastries and treats. This way, many more guests may come and enjoy the festival.

Yemenite children go to Hanukkah parties and bring roasted corn, carrots and grape juice.

In honor of Judith (see page 46) we also eat cheese blintzes, and stuff the latkes with sour cream or cottage cheese.

In Russia, Sufganiyot, the traditional Hanukkah donuts, are called "Pontshkes."

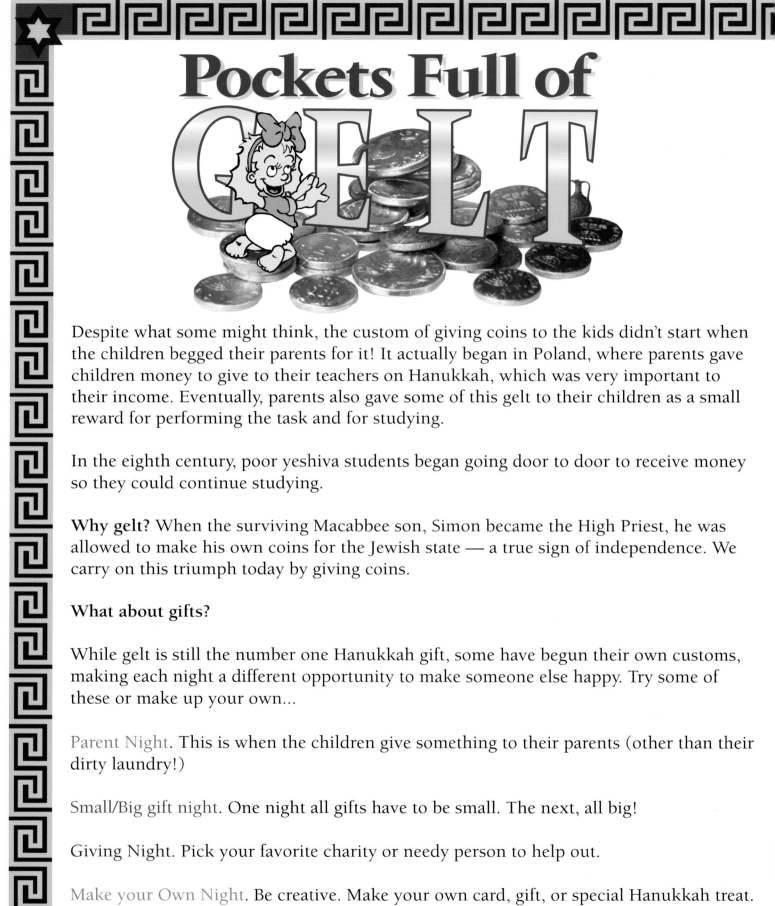

Pockets Full of GELT

Despite what some might think, the custom of giving coins to the kids didn't start when the children begged their parents for it! It actually began in Poland, where parents gave children money to give to their teachers on Hanukkah, which was very important to their income. Eventually, parents also gave some of this gelt to their children as a small reward for performing the task and for studying.

In the eighth century, poor yeshiva students began going door to door to receive money so they could continue studying.

Why gelt? When the surviving Macabbee son, Simon became the High Priest, he was allowed to make his own coins for the Jewish state — a true sign of independence. We carry on this triumph today by giving coins.

What about gifts?

While gelt is still the number one Hanukkah gift, some have begun their own customs, making each night a different opportunity to make someone else happy. Try some of these or make up your own...

Parent Night. This is when the children give something to their parents (other than their dirty laundry!)

Small/Big gift night. One night all gifts have to be small. The next, all big!

Giving Night. Pick your favorite charity or needy person to help out.

Make your Own Night. Be creative. Make your own card, gift, or special Hanukkah treat.

In Poland, Hassidic Jews used to collect clothing, food and wood and deliver to the poor with enough supplies for the year.

In Kurdistan, children carried dolls of Antiochus and asked for money. At the end of the day, they set the dolls on fire.

GIMME YOUR **CASH** OR YOUR DOLL IS **ASH!**

The 6th Night

In Jerusalem's Sephardic schools, children go from house to house collecting food such as beans, onions, garlic and rice. They then dance with kettles on their heads at the synagogue before preparing a feast for orphans, widows and the poor. The children are rewarded with special meat pies.

While the eighth night represents the spiritual completion of the holiday, the number six denotes a physical completion: the creation of the world lasted six days, and a complete self-contained object, such as the Star of David, consists of six dimensions: above and below, right and left, before and behind.

NOW I KNOW WHY GROWN-UPS LOVE GOLD, POODLY... IT HAS CHOCOLATE IN IT!

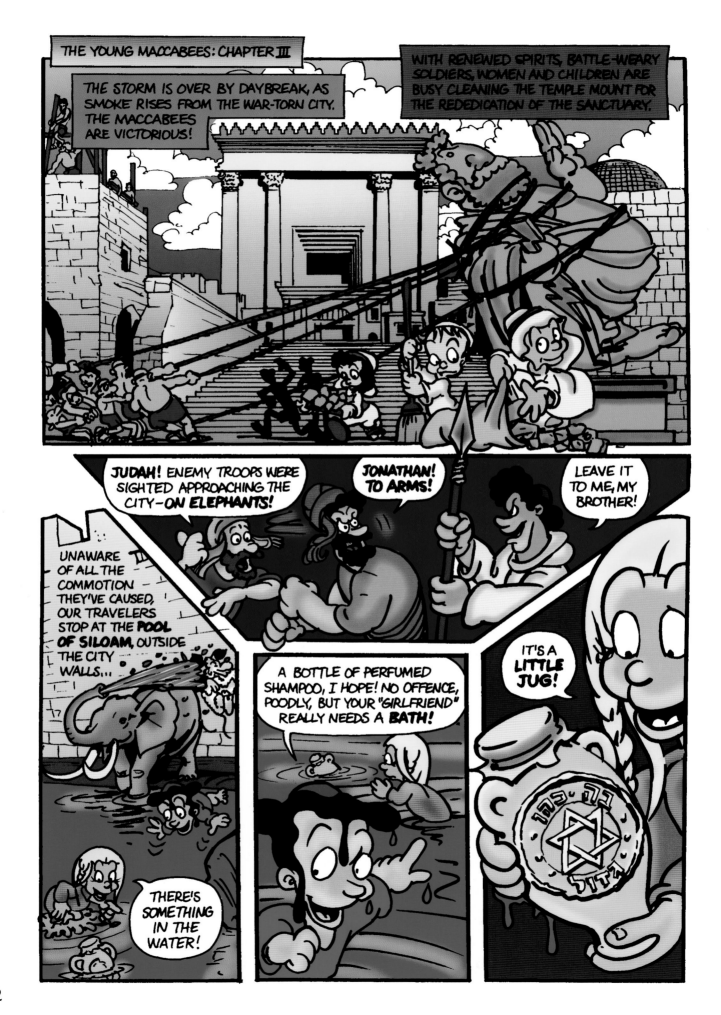

43

45

Although customs vary, the 7th and 8th nights were dedicated in honor of Jewish women, and they were excused from working on these nights. In fact, while the candles are burning, no one may work.

In North Africa, women used to go to the synagogue on the seventh night and for the only time of the year, were permitted to hold the Torah scrolls.

In Tunisia, Rosh Chodesh Tevet is known as The New Moon of the Daughters and is a time when parents and spouses give gifts to their wives and daughters.

In Morocco, the women gather to tell stories every night of Hanukkah, while in Eastern Europe the women are free from working on the first and last nights.

The 7th Night

The Women of Hanukkah

Hannah and her seven sons chose death rather than worship idols as commanded by the emperor. When the cruel ruler felt pity for the 7th son and offered to drop his ring on the floor so the lad would have an excuse to bow down. Like his brothers and mother before him, he refused to bow to the idol and was executed.

Judith went to the Syrian general Holofernes' tent and brought him salty dairy foods which made him drink a lot of wine. When he passed out, she beheaded him, causing his soldiers to panic and flee. In honor of this great victory for the Jewish rebellion, the custom is to eat cheese blintses and other dairy foods on Hanukkah.

Maccabee women baked pancakes and brought them to their husbands on the battlefields. Latkes were a favorite even back then!

The number eight is special in many ways... It's the day for Brit (circumcision). First born animals are dedicated to G-d on their eighth day. While seven is considered a perfect, complete number, eight is beyond completion and time - it signifies the Eternal. Before a sanctuary can be dedicated it must undergo a seven day purification, and the eighth day is the *Hanukkaht Habayit*.

In Hebron, the women used to hold a special celebration on the last night and eat macaroni and salty cheese, spending the evening talking and telling stories.

In Morocco, Jewish people didn't talk or eat on the last day of Hanukkah to make up for anything they may have said that wasn't nice. Similarly, the Breslov Hassidim believe that by kindling the Hanukkah lights, we banish strife and malicious slander.

The 8th Night

ELEPHANT STORIES

What do elephants have to do with Hanukkah?

King Ptolemy Philopater wanted to enter the forbidden Holy of Holies. As he tried to force his way in, he instantly fell unconscious. Upon awakening, he was furious and ordered many of the Jews of Alexandria into the sports arena to be trampled by wild, drunken elephants. Instead, the beasts turned on the spectators, killing and injuring thousands. Ptolemy took this as a sure sign from heaven and decided to leave the Jews alone.

Later, during Syrian rule, Battle-trained elephants were used much in the same way as tanks are used in modern warfare. When general Lysias and the nine year old king, Antiochus Eupater, marched on Jerualem with a large army led by 32 elephants, Eleazar, the youngest Maccabee brother, sacrificed his life in order to turn around a losing battle. He fought his way to the largest and most decorated elephant whom he mistakenly thought carried the king, and thrusted his spear into its belly, causing himself to be crushed by the fallen elephant This courageus act and great sacrifice helped turn the battle around.

SEE YOU IN THE NEXT DOODLE FAMILY ADVENTURE!

Look for the **Doodle Family Haggadah** and other favorite Doodle tiltles in stores everywhere.

Check out **The Doodle Family** comic strips appearing in over 40 newspapers across America.

The author at work